Word Families Mini-Books

75 Reproducible Activity Books for the Most Common Word Families

Fun to color and learn!

Easy to cut and fold!

Mini-Books are **BIG** on fun!

Written by Audrey Prince, M.Ed. & Molly DeShong
Designed by Jessica L. Horton

Post Office Box 24997, Greenville, SC 29616 USA
Call Toll Free 1-800-277-8737 • Fax 1-800-978-7379
Online! www.superduperinc.com
E-Mail: custserv@superduperinc.com

Copyright © 2006 by SUPER DUPER® PUBLICATIONS. A division of Super Duper®, Inc. All rights reserved. Permission is granted for the user to reproduce the material contained herein in limited form for classroom use only. Reproduction of this material for an entire school or school system is strictly prohibited.

ISBN# 1-58650-621-8

Introduction

Fold and Say® Word Families Mini-Books has 75 reproducible Mini-Books to help children learn the common word families. Each Mini-Book includes six illustrations and writing practice for words in each word family. It also includes a CD-ROM to make printing the books quick and easy.

The workbook/CD-ROM set also includes reproducible beginning sound and word family cards. Students use the beginning sound (onset) and the ending sound (rime/word family) cards to make words that belong to the same word family.

For extra fun, have students color the black and white reproducible while they practice saying the words from each word family. Students may also take these Mini-Books home for practice and fun with their homework partner. *Fold and Say® Word Families Mini-Books* may be little, but they're BIG on fun!

Table of Contents

How to Make Your Mini-Book	iii
Word Family Activities	iv
Word Family Mini-Books	1-75

(-ab, -ack, -ad, -ag, -ail, -ain, -ake, -all, -am, -ame, -amp, -an, -and, -ank, -ap, -ar, -ark, -ash, -at, -ate, -ave, -aw, -ay, -ed, -eep, -eet, -ell, -en, -end, -ent, -est, -et, -ew, -ice, -ick, -id, -ide, -ig, -ill, -ime, -in, -ine, -ing, -ink, -ip, -it, -ive, -oat, -ob, -ock, -od, -og, -oil, -old, -ole, -one, -ool, -op, -ore, -ose, -ot, -ound, -out, -ow, -own, -ub, -uck, -ug, -um, -ump, -un, -unk, -ush, -ut, -ute)

Beginning Sound Cards (onsets)	76-77
Word Family Cards (rimes)	77-80
Bonus Pages & Awards	81-84

How to Make Your Mini-Book

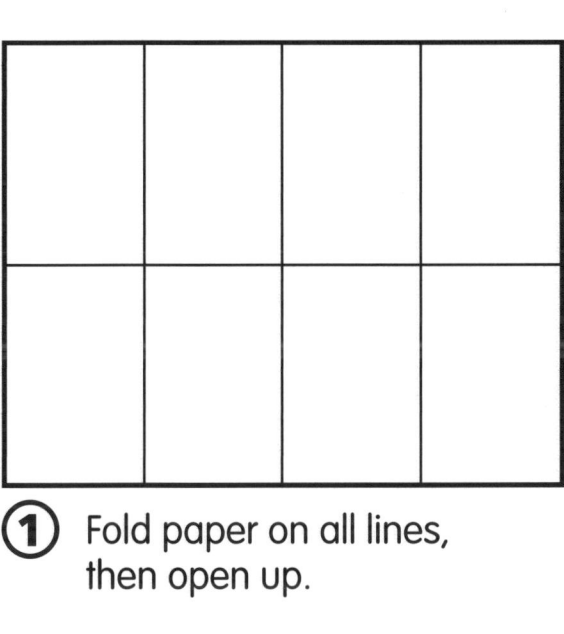

① Fold paper on all lines, then open up.

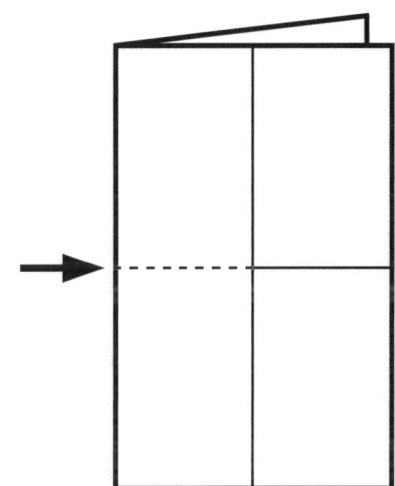

② Fold paper in half, then cut along the dotted line as shown above.

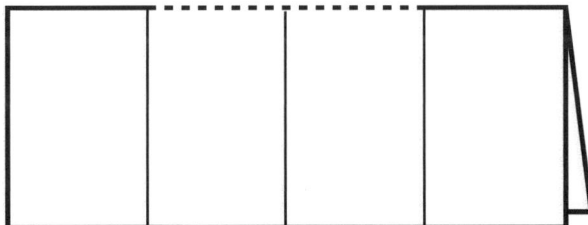

③ Open and fold lengthwise.

④ Push in on both ends.

⑤ Fold the book and close.

Word Families Activities

- Have children create their own word family books.

- Match words to pictures that are in the same word family.

- Write a word ending on the board (e.g., "-ave"). Children create as many words as they can using that ending.

- Create a word family web. Children write or glue pictures of words ending with a selected word family in a web. Example:

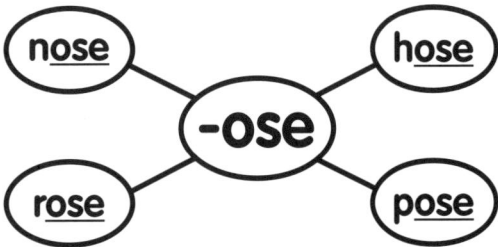

- Go for a "Sound Search." Have children go for a search around their classroom for objects that belong to the same word family. Record what the children find on the board. You can make this activity more exciting by putting the word endings in a grab bag. Children reach in the grab bag and pull out a word ending to begin their search.

- Go through books, and have the children listen/watch for words that belong to the same word family.

- Show and Tell for Word Families. Have children bring something with them to class that belongs to a particular word family.

- Group pictures of words that are in the same word family (e.g., pink, think, sink).

- Read out loud five words that belong to a particular word family. After reading the words, ask the child/children to guess the word family that all of the words belong to.

- Select five word families for a round of play. Write two columns of five words (in each column) on the board, with one word in each column from the five select word families. Have students match up the words in each column that belong to the same word family.

- Choose a word family and write the ending on the board. Set a timer and ask students to write down as many words as they can think of that belong to the word family on the board.

- Have children tell a silly story, using as many words as they can from a particular word family.

- Write several words from one word family on the board. Have students draw a line through the word to separate the beginning sound (onset) from the ending sound/word family (rime).

- Divide students into pairs. Give each pair a word family and have them take turns coming up with words from that word family. The students go back and forth until they can't think of any other word family words.

gab

3

grab
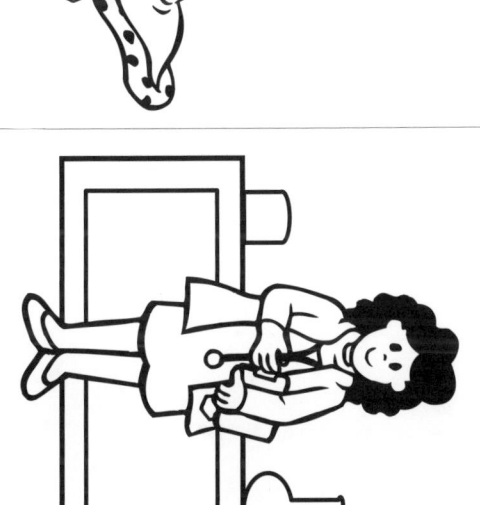
4

lab

5

dab

6

crab

2

cab

1

My Mini-Book by
_____

c l r d
7

snack

back

shack

crack

My Mini-Book by

sack

black

b__ __ __
sh__ __
bl__ __

mad

dad

lad

sad

My ___ Mini-Book by ___

glad

Chad

s   d   m

wag

brag

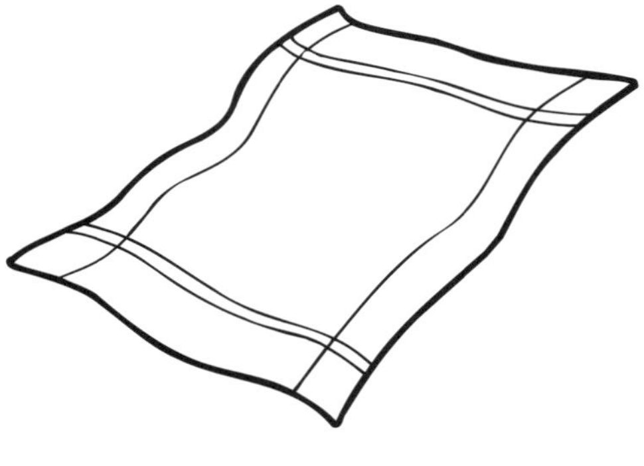

rag

tag

My Mini-Book by

_____

bag

r_____
w_____
b_____

flag

pail

3

nail

2

snail

4

mail

1

quail

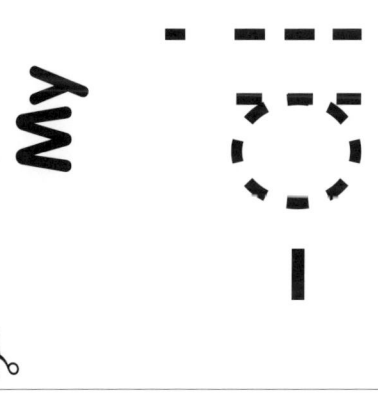

5

My **Mini-Book** by

_____

tail

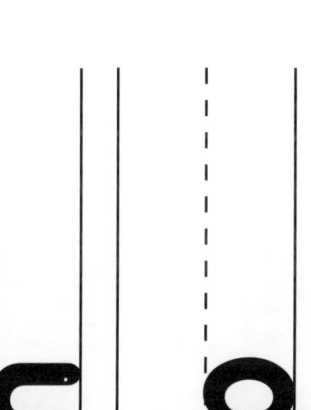

6

t
n
p

7

chain

brain

My ___ Mini-Book by

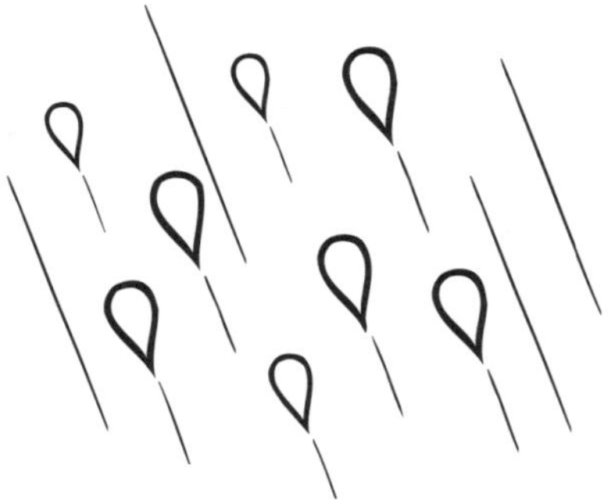

rain

train

drain

stain

r ___
tr ___
st ___

shake

snake

rake

lake
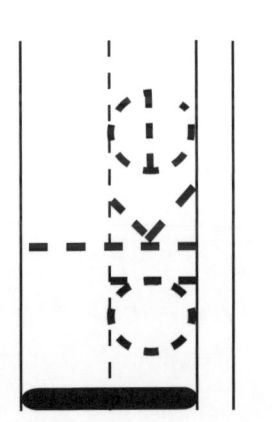

bake

cake
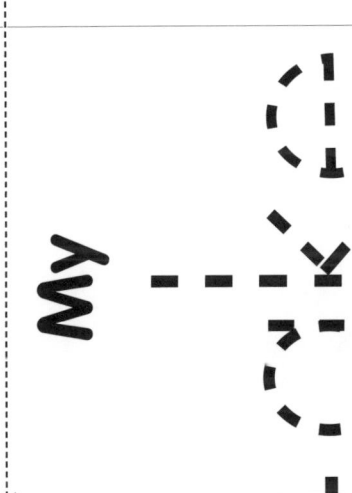

My _____ Mini-Book by _____

c a k e
b

My Mini-Book by ___

ball

mall

tall

wall

call

fall

b ___
f ___
t ___

ram

jam

clam

ham

swam

My _am_ Mini-Book by _____

slam

r___
h___
c___

game

flame

My ___ Mini-Book by ___

same

name

frame

tame

s___
g___
n___

clamp

lamp

stamp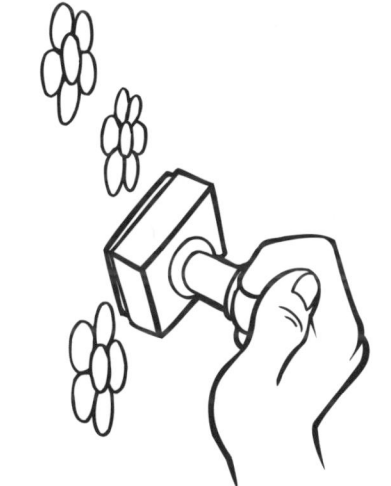

camp

champ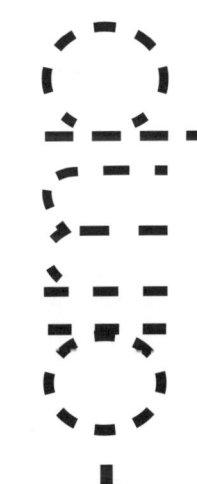

My Mini-Book by _____

ramp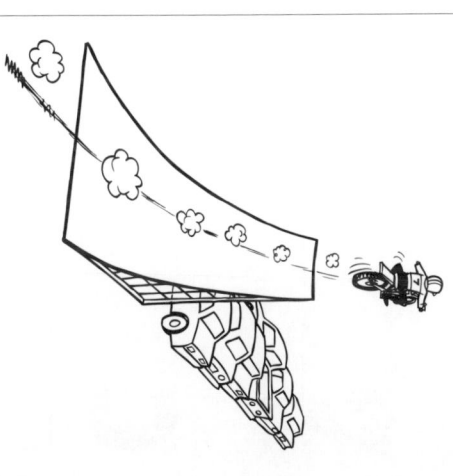

l___
c___
r___

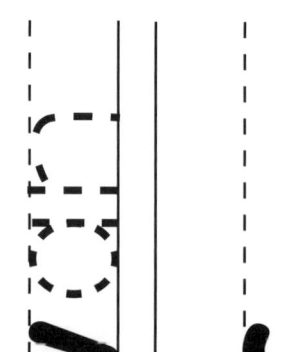
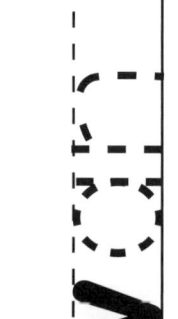
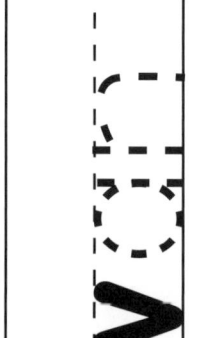

man

pan

My ___ Mini-Book by ___

van

fan

can

v___
c___
r___

ran

land

hand

sand

band

stand

My

Mini-Book by
_____

island

Page 3
drank

Page 2

stank

Page 4

tank

Page 1
bank

Page 5

plank

Cover
My _ank_ Mini-Book by _____

Page 6
yank

Page 7
ank, b___, st___

trap

nap

My **-i-** Mini-Book by _____

map

yap

lap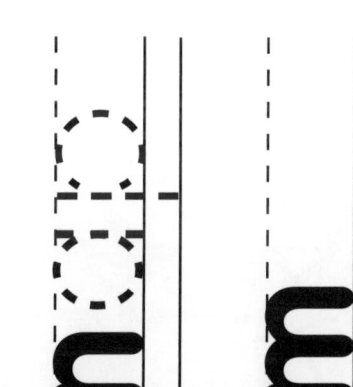

cap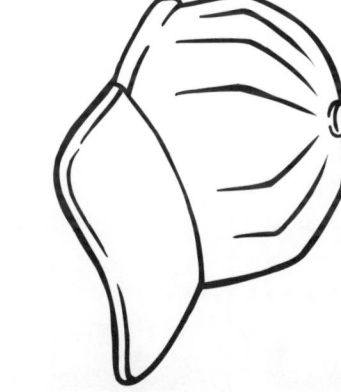

m ___ **-i-**n ___

st__ar__

c__ar__

f__ar__

j__ar__

t__ar__

My ☆
Mini-Book
by _____

sc__ar__

c __ __
f __ __
t __ __

dark

bark

park

shark

spark

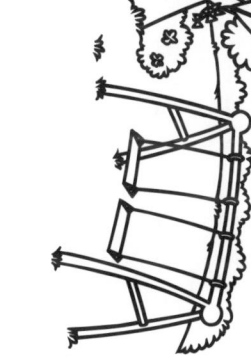

My 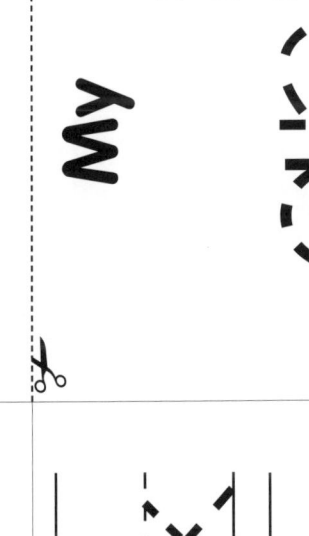 Mini-Book by
_____

lark

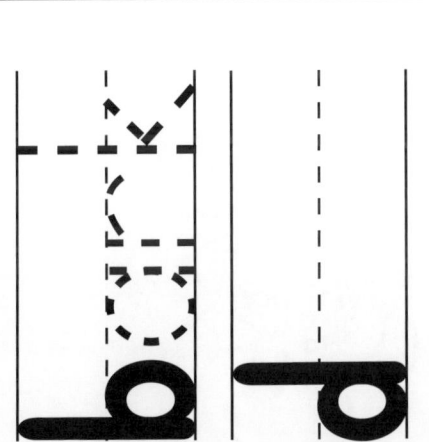

smash

2

cash

1

My _sh_ Mini-Book by _____

splash

3

trash

4

dash

5

crash

6

c a sh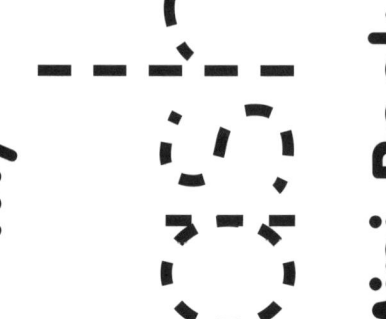
tr
d

7

hat

3

cat

2

mat

4

bat

1

fat

5

My
t
a
Mini-Book by
_____

sat

6

b
c
s
7

plate

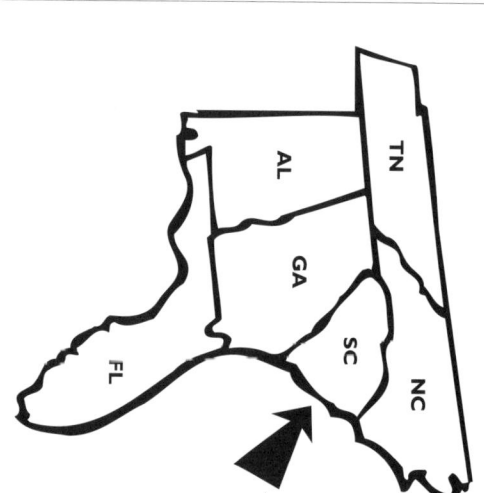

skate

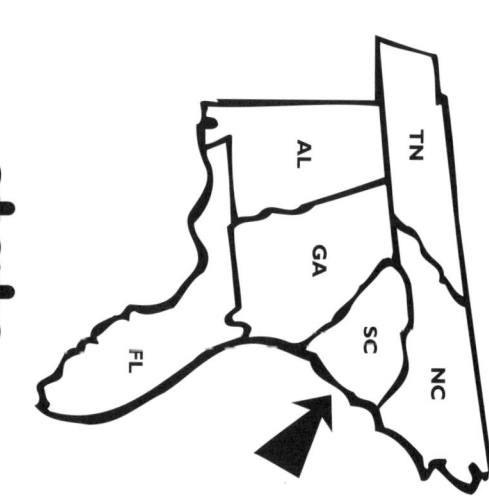

state

date

late

gate

My Mini-Book
by
_____

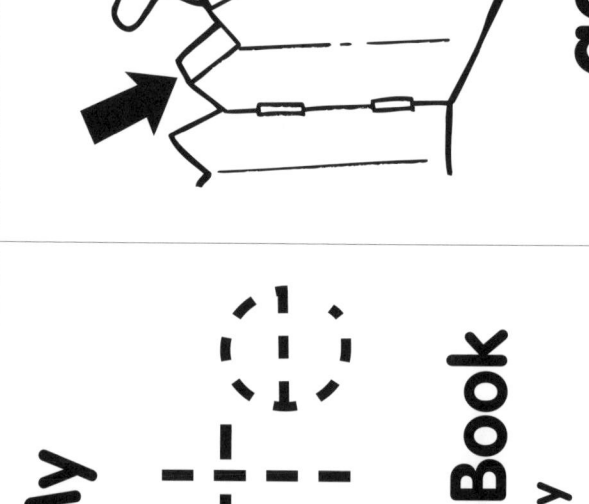
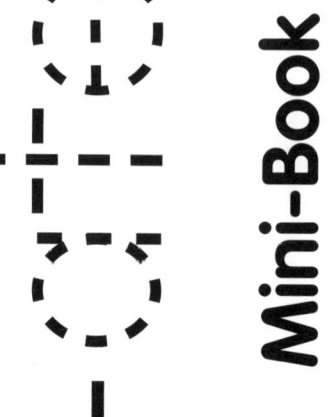
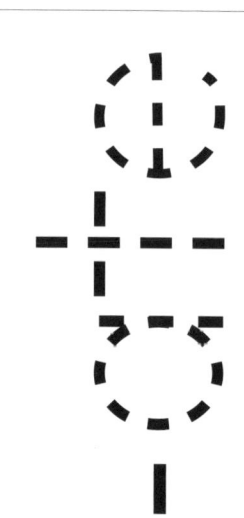

© 2006 Super Duper® Publications
1-800-277-8737 • www.superduperinc.com

grave

cave

---

wave

shave

---

brave

My _ _ _ _ Mini-Book by _____

---

save

C _ _ _ _
s _ _ _ _ _
w _ _ _ _

paw

3

draw

2

flaw

4

claw

1

straw

5

My Mini-Book by

saw

6

p _ _ _
s _ _ _ _
dr _ _

7

May

pay

stay

play

My āy Mini-Book by ___

stray

clay

pāy / clāy / stāy

My _ _ _ Mini-Book by _____

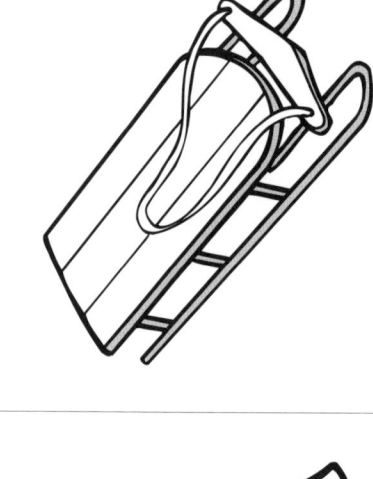
sled

2

shed

3

bed

1

wed

4

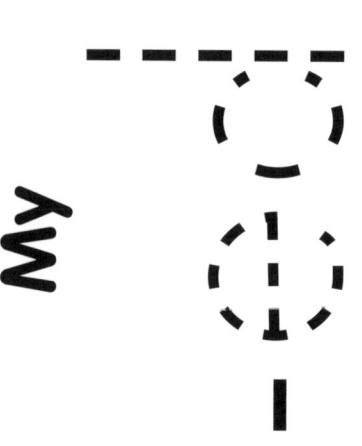
red

5

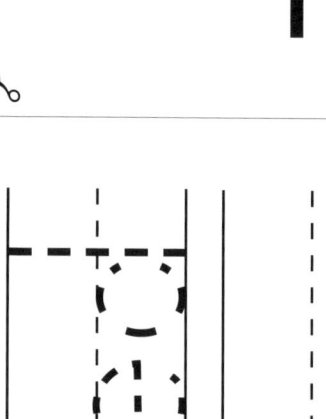
Ted

6

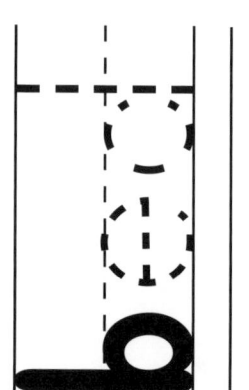
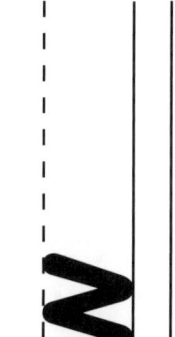
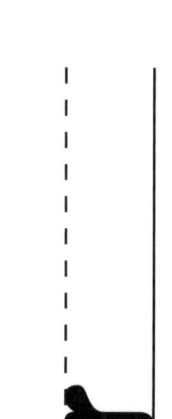

7

sheep

sleep

beep

sweep

My -ee- Mini-Book
by _____

deep

weep

b
d
w

My Mini-Book by _____

street

beet

sweet

tweet!

fleet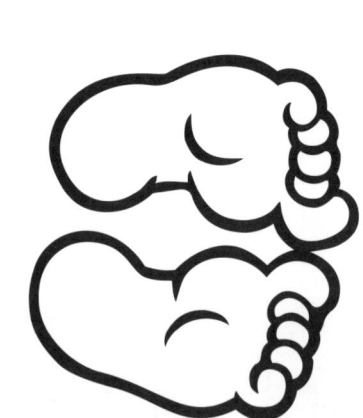

feet

well

bell

Mini-Book by
My ____
____

smell
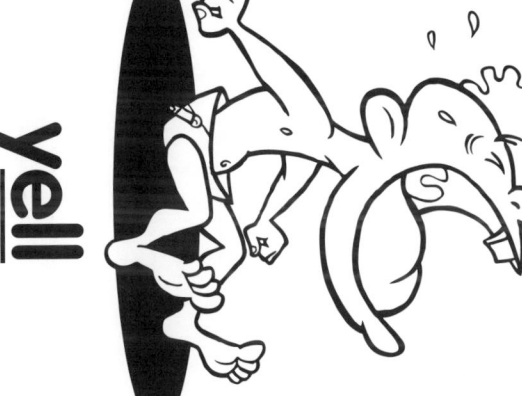

yell

sell
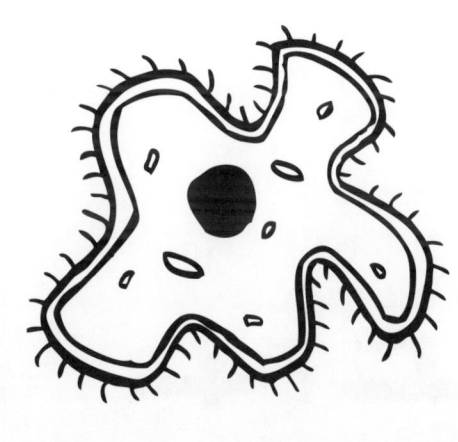

cell
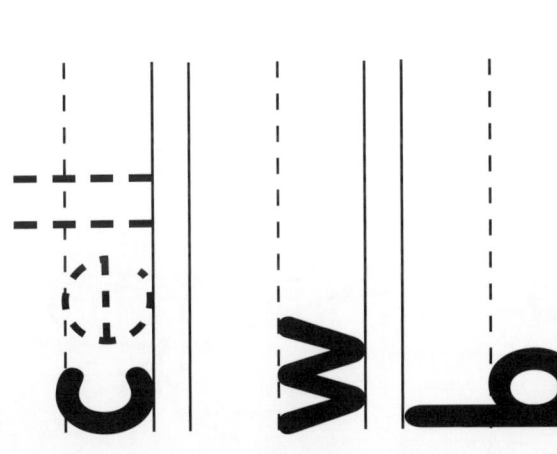

c ____
w ____
b ____

ten

pen

den

hen

men

My  Mini-Book by

_____

Ben

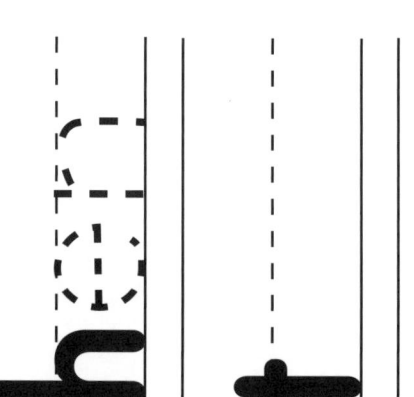

friend

2

bend

1

send

3

spend

4

lend

5

My Mini-Book by
_____

mend

6

7

My Mini-Book

by
_____

1
cent

2
gent

3
bent

4
rent

5
tent
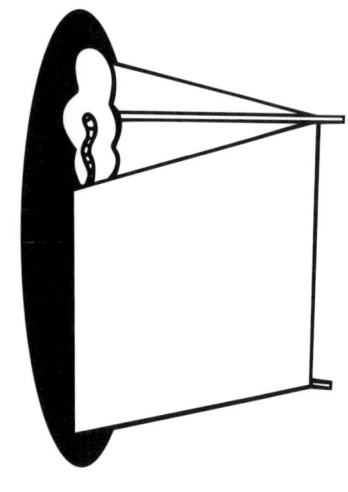

6
sent

7
t _ _ _
c _ _ _
r _ _ _

Page 3
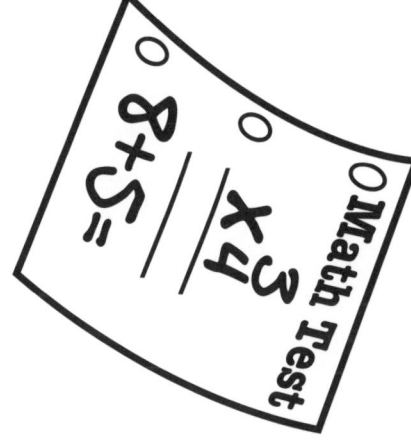
test

Page 2
vest

Page 4

west

Page 1
nest

Page 5
chest

My  Mini-Book by
_____

Page 6
rest

Page 7
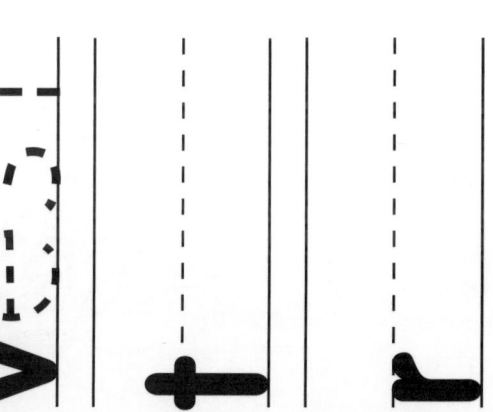

My Mini-Book
by _____

net 2

jet 1

pet 3

set 4

wet 5

met 6

-e-t
-e-n
-e-w
-e-m
7

crew

drew

chew

new

My ___ Mini-Book
by
_____

stew

bl___

n e w
cr __
bl __

blew

spice

3

rice

2

price
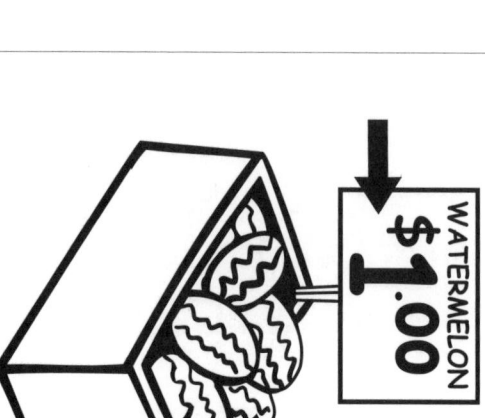
4

mice

1

dice

5

My **i** Mini-Book by

slice
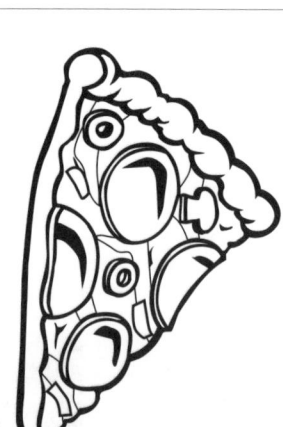
6

7

r **i**

m

p

lick

kick
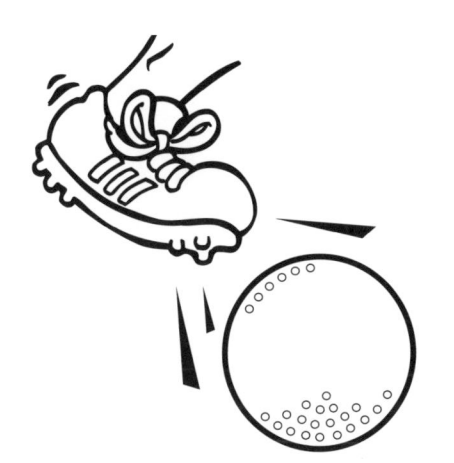

chick
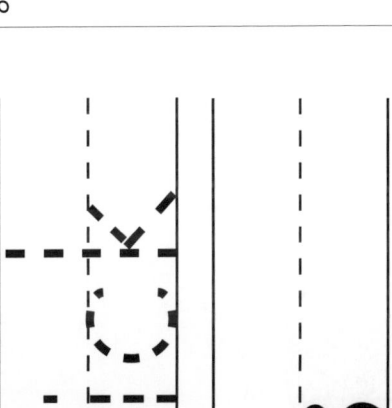

sick

My ick Mini-Book by
_____

stick

lick
sick
kick

pick

lid

kid

My
Mini-Book
by
_____

slid

hid

grid

skid

l k h

bride

ride

slide

hide

glide

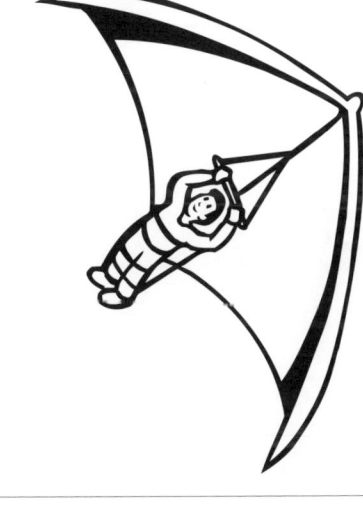

My _ i _ _
Mini-Book by
_____

wide

h i _ _
r _ _ _
w _ _ _

big

pig

dig

wig

My  Mini-Book by
_____

twig

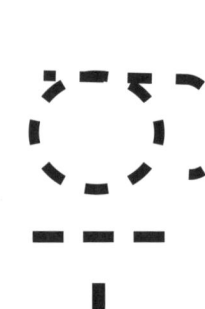

rig

drill

pill

Mini-Book by _____

My _____

hill

spill

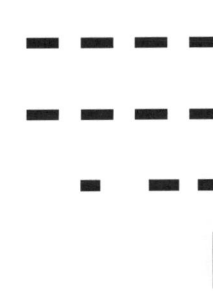

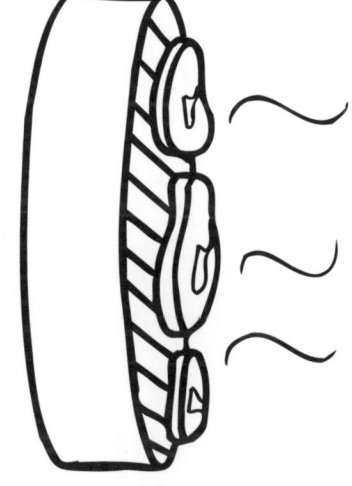

grill

h b p

bill

time

dime

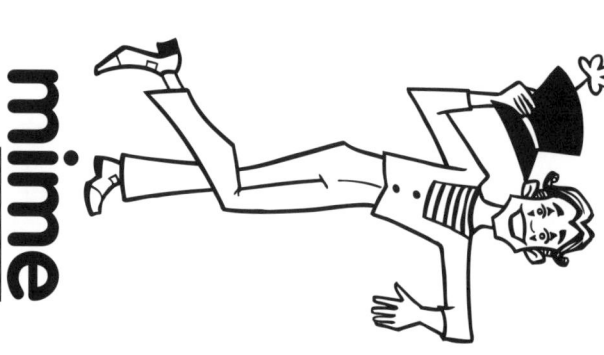

mime

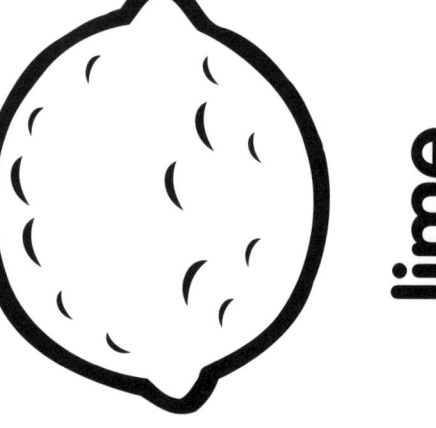

lime

slime

My ime Mini-Book by

chime

lime
dime
time

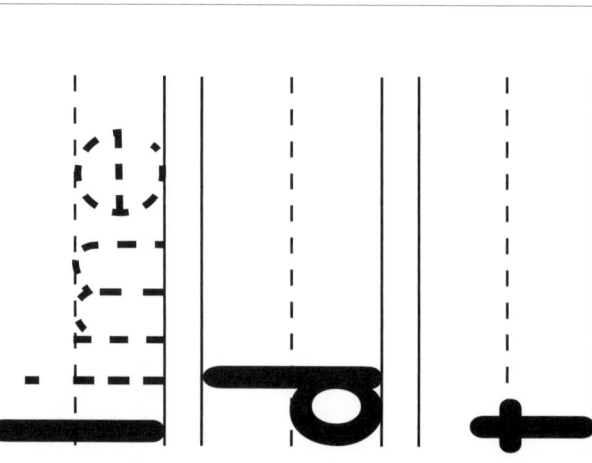

My "in" Mini-Book by
_____

chin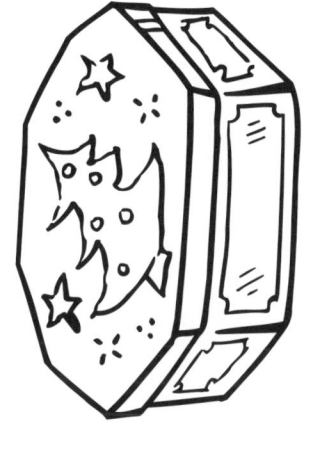

tin

spin

twin

win

fin

t_ _ _
w_ _
f_ _

2

nine

3

sh**ine**

1

m**ine**

My ___ Mini-Book by ___

4

v**ine**

5

l**ine**

7

n i n e

6

d**ine**

king

sing

ring

string

My Mini-Book
by
_____

swing

r ing
s ing
w ing

wing

Page 2
ink

Page 3
think

Page 1
pink

Page 4
drink

My -ink Mini-Book by ___

Page 5
stink

Page 6
sink

Page 7
p_ink_
s_ink_
st_ink_

tip

trip

drip

chip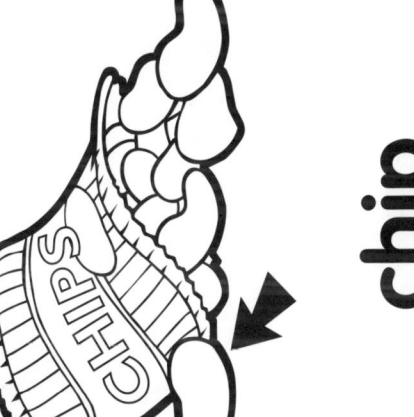

ship

My **ip** Mini-Book by _____

rip

t **ip**
r ___
sh ___

sit

fit

mitt

bit

chomp!

split

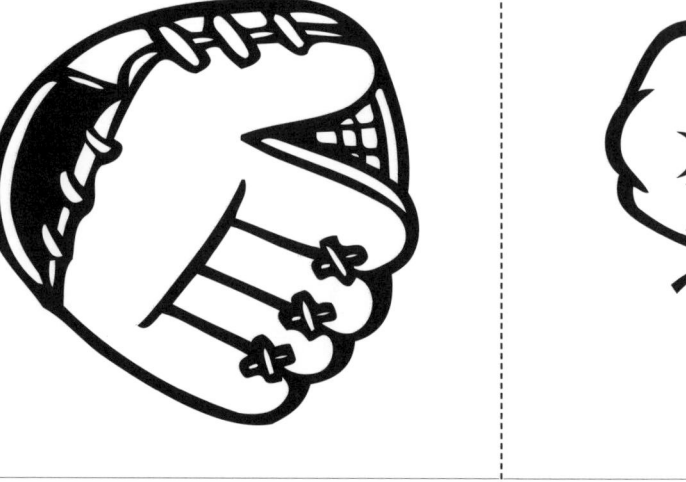

My

Mini-Book

by

_____

hit

s

f

p

hive

5
five

drive

dive

alive

My **-ive**

Mini-Book by
_____

arrive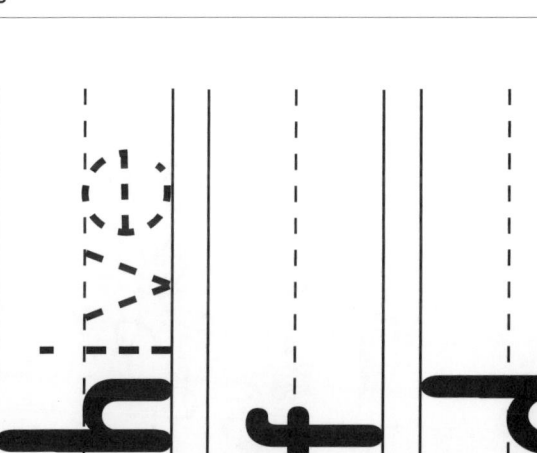

h **ive**
f ___
d ___

coat

2

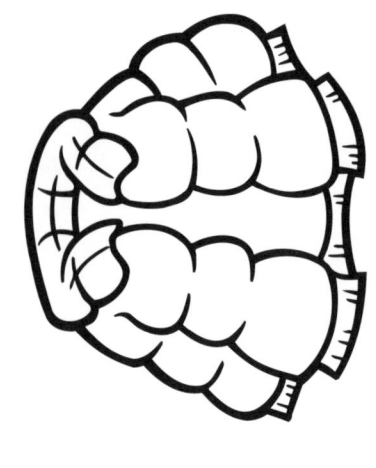

boat

1

---

goat

3

throat

4

---

float

5

moat

6

My

t o

Mini-Book by

_____

 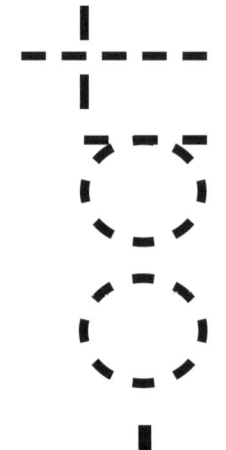 

t g c

7

sob

mob

cob

job

knob

My _ _ _ _

Mini-Book
by
_____

slob

c _ _
s _ _
m _ _

Page 2
sock

Page 1
rock

Page 3
lock

Page 4
dock

Page 5
clock

Cover
My **-ock** Mini-Book by _____

Page 6
block

Page 7
s ___
r ___
l ___

My Mini-Book by _____

pod

nod

rod

sod

cod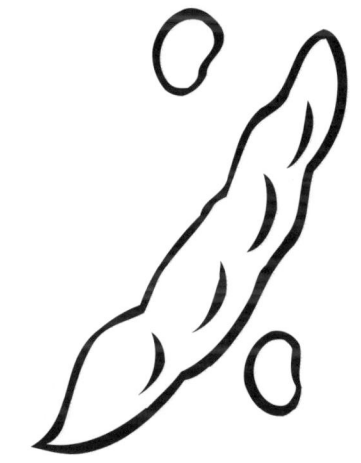

s____
r____
n____

hot rod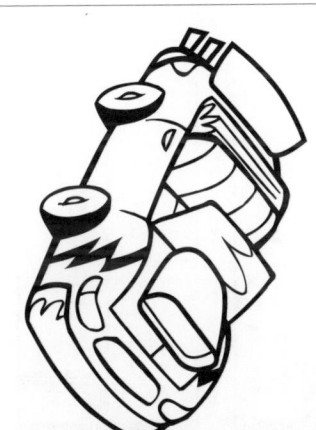

hog

jog

dog

log

Mini-Book by

My

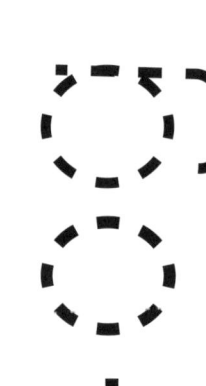

frog

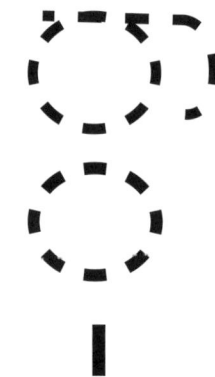

d
h
l

clog

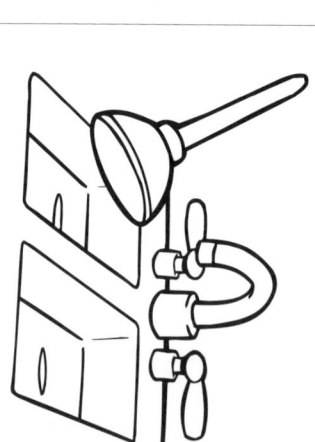

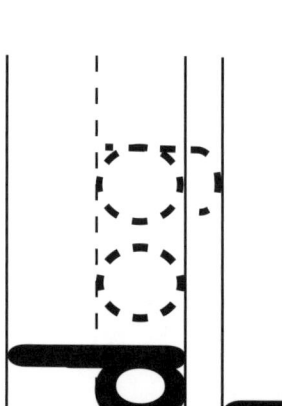

2
foil
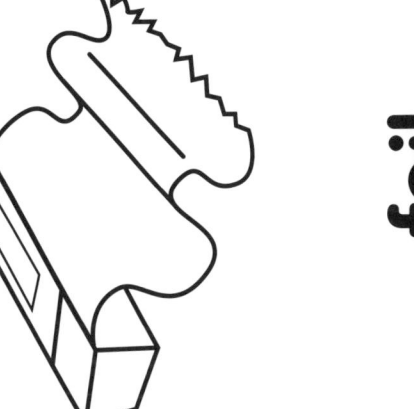

3
soil

1
oil
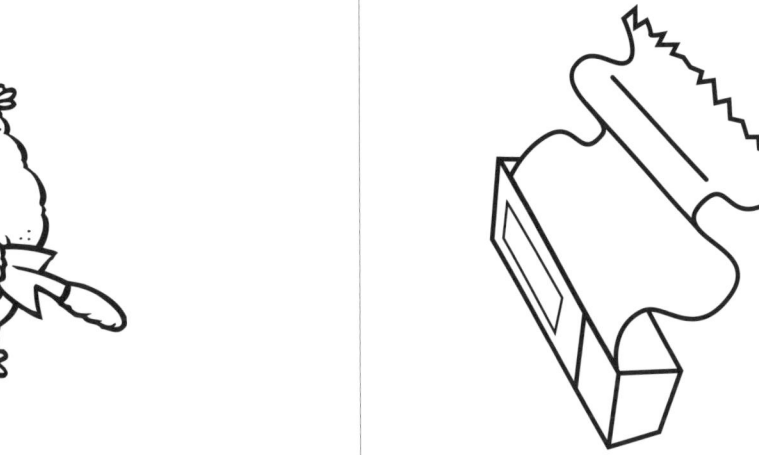

My Mini-Book by
_____
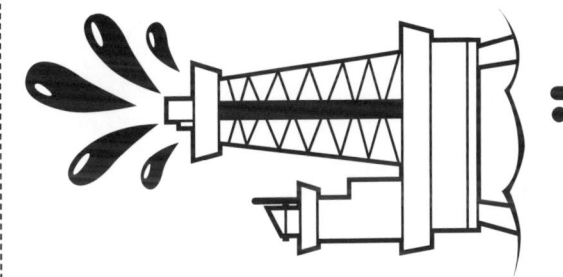

4
boil

5
coil

7
f___
s___
b___
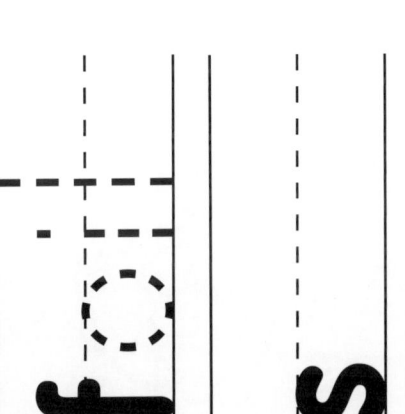

6
spoil

My _____ Mini-Book by _____

gold

old

cold

sold

hold

told

2
pole

3
hole

1
mole

4
role

My Mini-Book by
_____

5
sole

6
stole
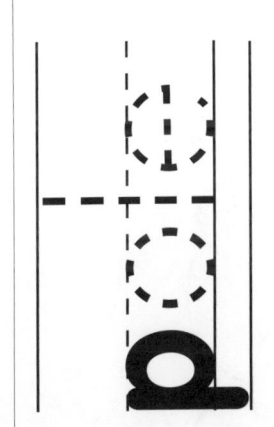

7

bone

cone

stone

throne

phone

alone

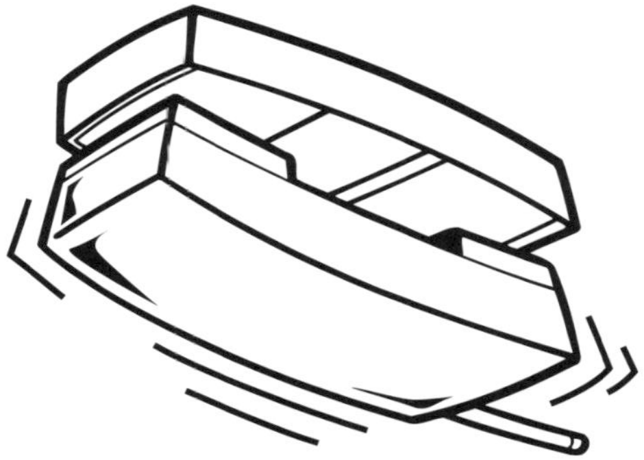

My ____ Mini-Book by ____

c _ _ _
b _ _ _
d _ _ _

tool

pool

My _oo_ Mini-Book
by
_____

cool

spool
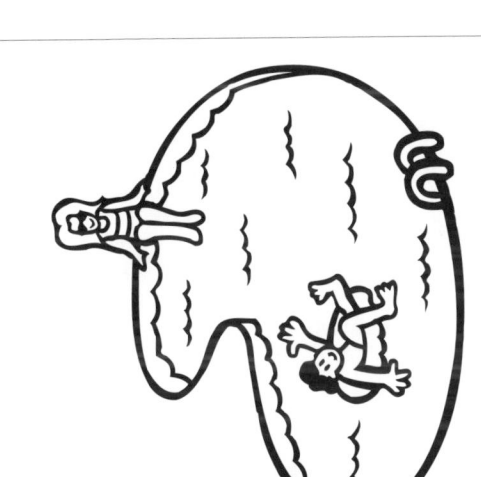

drool
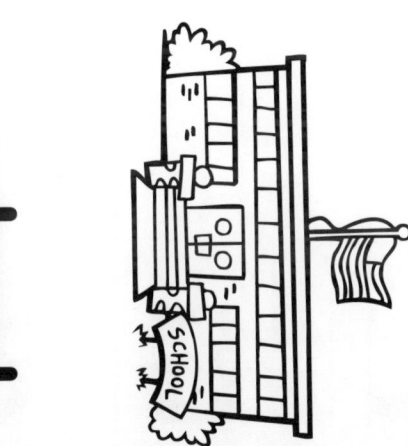

school
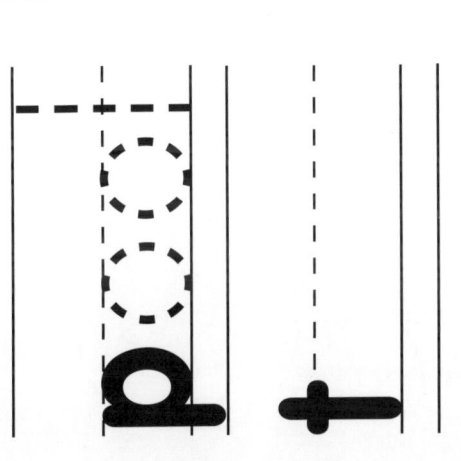

p___
t___
c___

top

mop

cop

stop

My  Mini-Book by _____

pop

shop

c _____
m _____
t  _____

store

tore

snore

more

score

My  Mini-Book by
_____

core

m___
c___
sc___

nose

rose
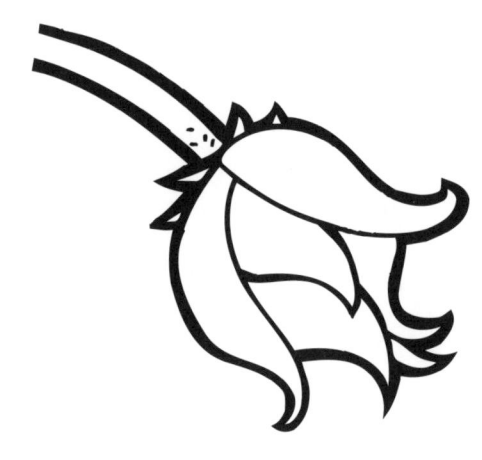

hose

chose

My _____ Mini-Book by _____

close
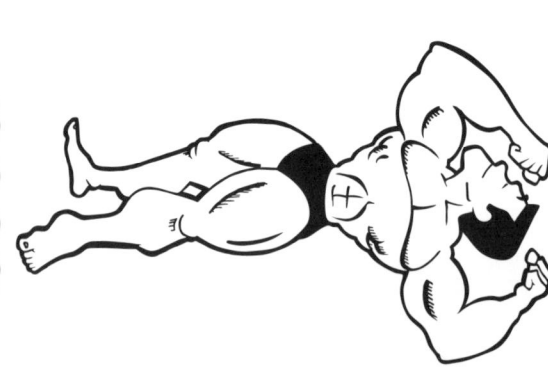

pose
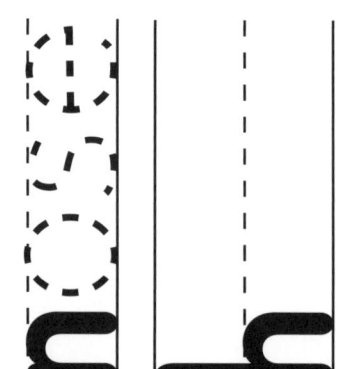

n o s e
h _ _ _
r _ _ _

hot

dot

pot

blot

knot

My _ot Mini-Book by _____

spot

_ot
p_ _ot
b_ _ot
h_ _ot

round
3
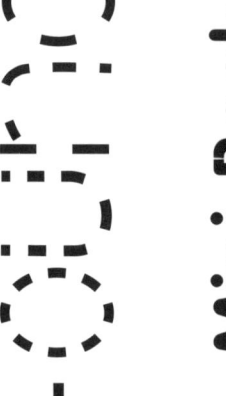

mound
2

found
1

bound
4

My Mini-Book by
_____

hound
5

sound
6
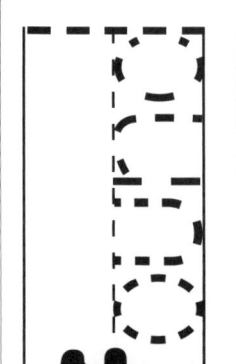

7
f o u n d
r
h

scout

shout

sprout

out

pout

My ___

Mini-Book by ___

snout

p___
sn___
sc___

Page 2
mow

Page 1
row

My "ow" Mini-Book by ___

Page 3
bow

Page 4
grow

Page 7
m ow
b ow
r ow

Page 5
throw

Page 6
snow
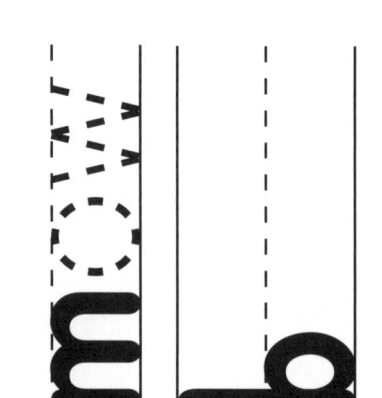

gown

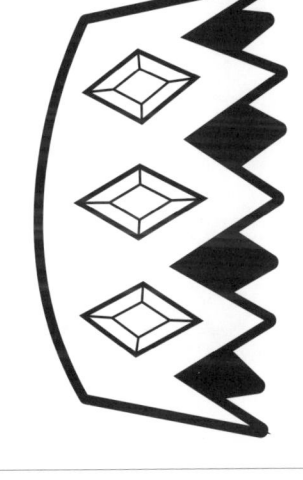

town

crown

down

clown

My

o w n

Mini-Book
by

_____

frown

t _____

d _____

g _____

sub

cub

My Mini-Book
by

rub

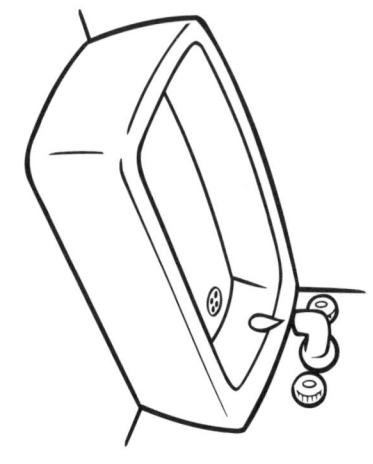

tub

club

scrub

c _ _ _

s _ _

r _ _

duck

truck

puck

buck

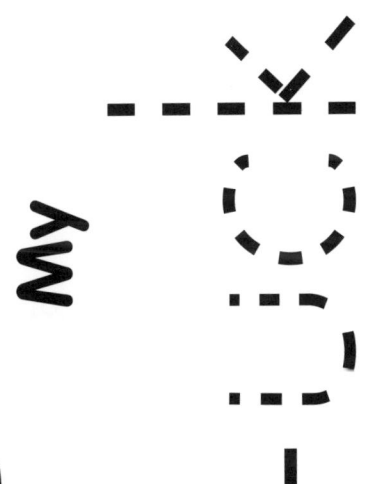

My ___ Mini-Book by ___

muck

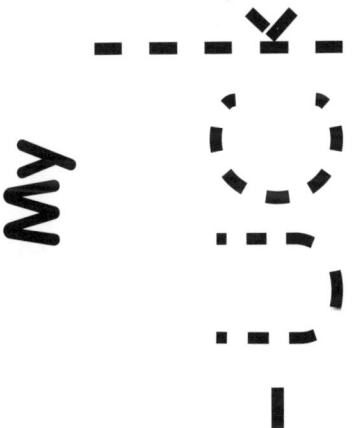

p   p   b

cluck

Page 2

mug

Page 3

tug

Page 1

bug

Page 4

hug

Title Page

My Mini-Book by _____

Page 5

rug

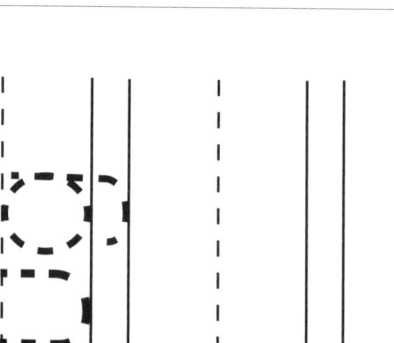

Page 6

jug

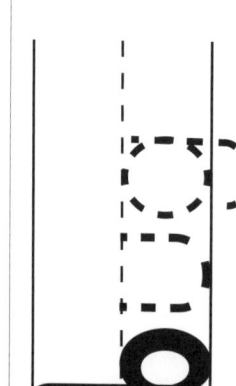

Page 7

b _ _
r _ _
t _ _

gum

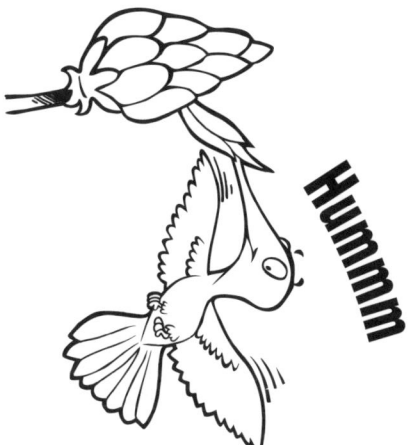

hum

Hummmm

sum

drum

My  Mini-Book by
_____

chum

s h g

strum

pump

3

jump

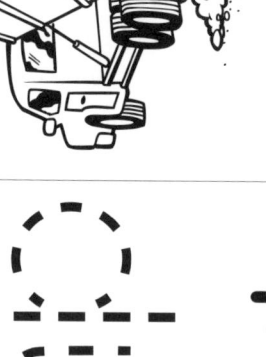

1

dump

2

bump

4

My _____
Mini-Book
by _____

lump

5

j p l

7

stump

6

sun

bun

fun

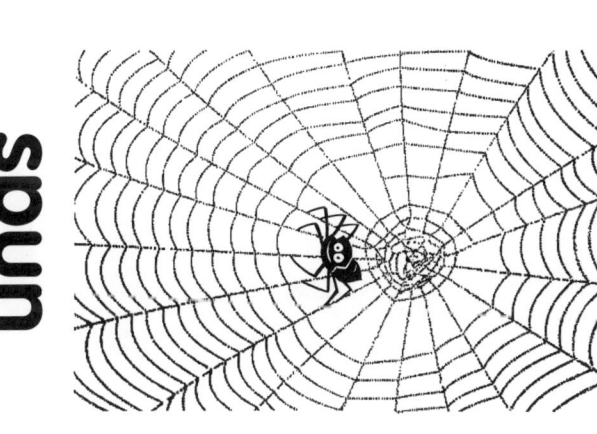

run

spun

My ___
Mini-Book
by ___

stun

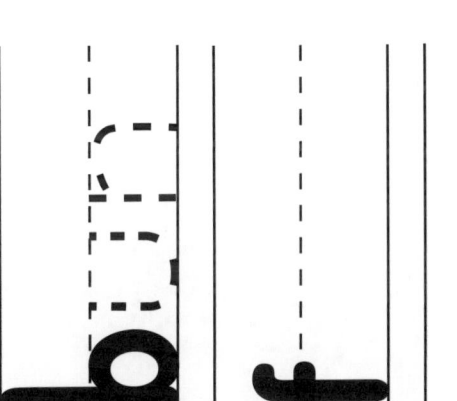

b ___
f ___
s ___

stunk

dunk

bunk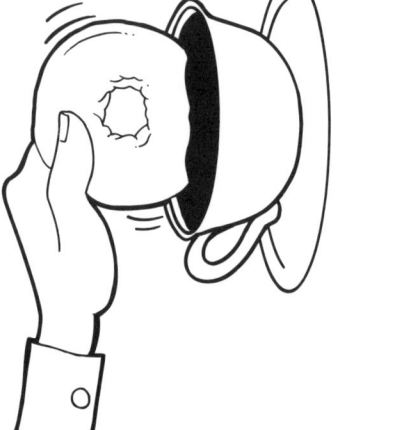

My Mini-Book by ___

junk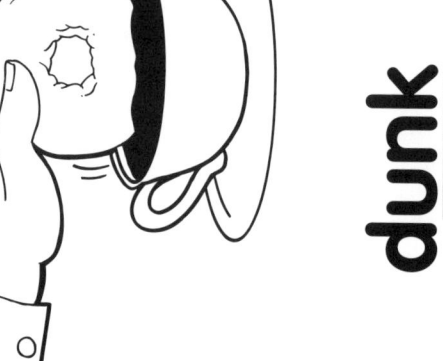

trunk

s_ _ _ _ j_ _ _ _ d_ _ _ _ b_ _ _ _

skunk

mush

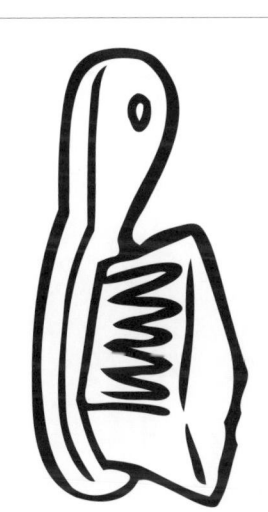

hush

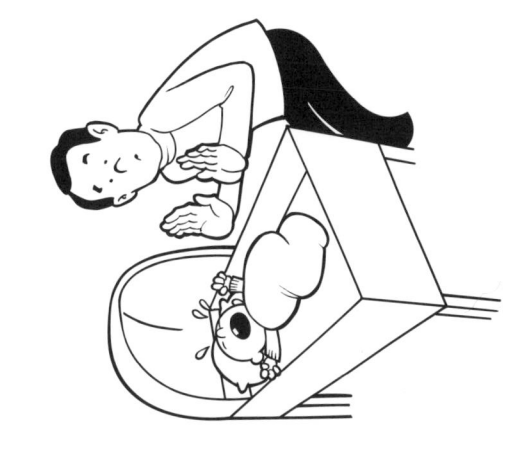

gush

rush

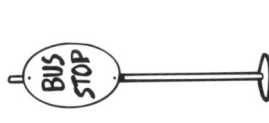

brush

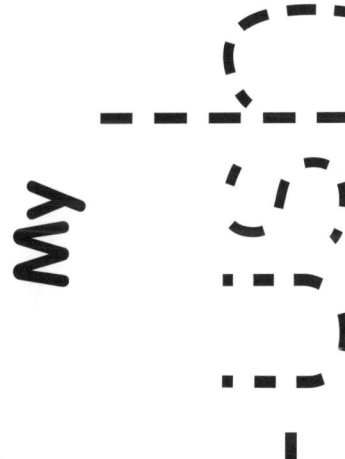

My List
Mini-Book
by
_____

crush

g_ _ _ _ _ _ _
r_ _ _ _ _ _ _
h_ _ _ _ _ _ _

My "u" Mini-Book

by
_____

nut

cut

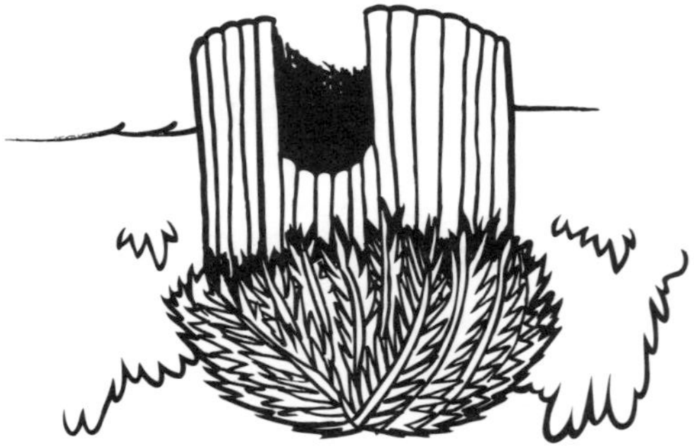

rut

hut

shut

strut

c u t

chute

flute

salute

cute

My _ _ _ _ Mini-Book by _____

dispute

"That's my ball." "No, it's not."

pollute

c _ _ _
ch _
f _

© 2006 Super Duper® Publications
1-800-277-8737 • www.superduperinc.com

b	c	d	f
g	h	j	k
l	m	n	p
q	r	s	t
v	w	x	y
z	bl	br	ch
cr	dr	fr	gr

kn	pl	pr	sc
sh	sk	sl	sn
st	th	tr	wh

-ab	-ack	-ad
-ag	-ail	-ain
-ake	-all	-am
-ame	-amp	-an

-and	-ank	-ap
-ar	-ark	-ash
-at	-ate	-ave
-aw	-ay	-ed
-eep	-eet	-ell
-en	-end	-ent
-est	-et	-ew

-ice	-ick	-id
-ide	-ig	-ill
-ime	-in	-ine
-ing	-ink	-ip
-it	-ive	-oat
-ob	-ock	-od
-og	-oil	-old

-ole	-one	-ool
-op	-ore	-ose
-ot	-ound	-out
-ow	-own	-ub
-uck	-ug	-um
-ump	-un	-unk
-ush	-ut	-ute

Way To Go
with Word Families

You're Swinging High with

_____

Skills!

Put gr with eat

Your word family skills are great!

_____
Student's Name

Is On The Road
to Reading and Writing Success

Name _____

Date _____